MW00510617

Breville Smart Air Fryer Oven Cookbook 2021

300 Healthy Recipes To Effortlessly Prepare Yummy Meals Including Breakfast, Lunch And Dinner With Your Air Fryer Oven

Table of Contents

© Copyright 2021 by Adele T. Cook - All rights reserved.The following Book is reproduced below with the goal of providing information that is as accurate and reliable as possible. Regardless, purchasing this Book can be seen as consent to the fact that both the publisher and the author of this book are in no way experts on the topics discussed within and that any recommendations or suggestions that are made herein are for entertainment purposes only. Professionals should be consulted as needed prior to undertaking any of the action endorsed herein.This declaration is deemed fair and valid by both the American Bar Association and the Committee of Publishers Association and is legally binding throughout the United States. Furthermore, the transmission, duplication, or reproduction of any of the following work including specific information will be considered an illegal act irrespective of if it is done electronically or in print. This extends to creating a secondary or tertiary copy of the work or a recorded copy and is only allowed with the express written consent from the Publisher. All additional right reserved.The information in the following pages is broadly considered a truthful and accurate account of facts and as such, any inattention, use, or misuse of the information in question by the reader will render any resulting actions solely under their purview. There are no scenarios in which the publisher or the original author of this work can be in any fashion deemed liable for any hardship or damages that may befall them after undertaking information described herein.

Additionally, the information in the following pages is intended only for informational purposes and should thus be thought of as universal. As befitting its nature, it is presented without assurance regarding its prolonged validity or interim quality. Trademarks that are mentioned are done without written consent and can in no way be considered an endorsement from the trademark holder.

Introduction

Are you looking for a new smart Air Fryer oven that will help you cook all sorts of meals? Well, you are about to get lucky, as we are introducing you to the amazing Breville Smart Air Fryer Oven. We all know Breville due to its variety of kitchen appliances. From the first toasted, they presented to the latest Air Fryer ovens; all came with quality and durability offered by Breville. As of today, there is a range of innovations that Breville introduced in the tech world. The smartest Breville Smart Air Fryer Oven is proven to be the most successful model of this range due to its smart features. In this air fryer oven cookbook, you can learn all about the Breville smart Air Fryer Oven and will get to know various recipes that you can cook using its smart cooking functions.

Benefits of Using Breville Smart Air Fryer Oven

1. *Space Friendly Design:*

The design of the Air Fryer oven is something that makes it stand out among the rest of the air fryer ovens in the market. It's size and shape make a complete balance; you can manage cooking space and your countertop space at the same time. Since this oven can replace multiple food appliances due to a variety of its cooking functions, it can be easily placed and set anywhere in the kitchen.

2. *13 Cooking Functions:*

This one appliance can replace most of the cooking appliances in your kitchen as it provides a number of cooking functions in one place. This Air Fryer oven can be used to bake food, toast, grill, roast, cookies, broil, and dehydrate all sorts of food items. The versatility of its cooking function increases when you count the temperature and timer settings, which can also be adjusted manually to cook according to your own preferences. There are several accessories that come with the oven, and they all help to cook on a specific cooking mode.

3. *Large Capacity:*

The Breville Air fryer oven is known for its large size and all the capacity suitable for cooking all portion sizes. So, whether you have one large family or a small family, this Air fryer oven can serve the needs of all. Now baking a 14 pounds turkey and roasting a whole chicken or a duck is not a problem, as you can not only adjust them all in this Air Fryer oven, but you can also add side ingredients along with them.

4. *Smart Control Panel and Crisping Technology:*

Another good feature of this Air Fryer oven is its easy and simple control panel, which is completely user friendly. The control dial is used to select the mode of cooking in each option.

Breville Smart Air Fryer Oven Deconstructed

When you unbox the appliance, you will find the following parts and components inside:

- The main cooking unit
- Air fry basket
- Baking dish
- Wire rack
- Crumb tray
- Dehydrator tray

All these accessories are dishwasher safe, can be removed and washed after the cooking session.

Control Panel and Cooking Functions:

The control panel is fixed on the front of the appliance, on top. And it has a dial, five buttons, and a display screen. On this screen, you can see all the presets written on the screen indicating different cooking functions:

- Bagel
- Toast
- Air fry
- Bake
- Roast
- Broil
- Cookies
- Pizza
- Reheat

How to use Breville Smart Air Fryer Oven

Here are a few simple steps to use your Breville Smart Air Fryer Oven:

1. *Getting Started:*

At first, place the appliance at an appropriate place in the kitchen. The back and top of the oven should be kept open for ventilation. Check all its accessories and then plug it in. The lights of the display screen will light up.

If you are using the oven for the first time, make sure to wash all the accessories with water or soap water and allow them to dry, and keep them at a place where they are safe from the dirt and grease.

2. *Setting Up the oven:*

The crumb tray is placed at the bottom of the oven, and it is important to use this tray to protect the floor of the oven. So always fix the crumb tray in the lowermost portion of the oven. You can now select the accessories according to the recipe and the type of food. The air fryer basket is used to Air Fry a variety of food items, so use this basket to keep the food inside the oven.

3. *Cooking and Adjustment:*

Now that you have selected the desired accessories for cooking. Prepare your food and keep it ready for the oven. The oven quickly attains the required heat for cooking, so it is suggested not to preheat the oven and directly place the food inside and then select the cooking functions. You can then adjust the settings according to the given recipe. Generally, it is best to select after your food is placed inside.

Cleaning and Maintenance

Unplug the appliance and remove all the trays or pans placed inside. Make sure to wear gloves or oven mittens while handling the hot trays. It is important to clean the tray and pan while they are hot to prevent all the grease and food particles stuck on them from hardening.

1. Leave the cooking appliance with its door open and allow it to cool completely.

2. Use this time to wash all the accessories used in the cooking operation. You can either wash them by lightly rub them with soap water or wash them in the dishwasher. Avoid using hard material to scrub these accessories, as they could damage their outer surface.

3. Now that the oven is cooled from inside out, you can take a lightly damp cloth and wipe off all the grease and food particles from the inner walls of the Air Fryer oven.

4. Use another lightly wet cloth to wipe off the doors, door handle, the control panel dial, its buttons, and the displace screen.

5. Never immerse the unit water and keep it away from liquids as well.

Breakfast Recipes

Oats, Nuts & Seeds Granola

Servings: 8

Preparation Time: 15 minutes

Cooking Time: 15 minutes

Ingredients:

- 1/3 cup olive oil

- ¼ cup maple syrup

- 2 tablespoons honey

- ½ teaspoon vanilla extract

- 2 cups rolled oats

- ½ cup wheat germ, toasted

- ¼ cup dried cherries

- ¼ cup dried blueberries

- 2 tablespoons dried cranberries

- 2 tablespoons sunflower seeds

- 2 tablespoons pumpkin seeds, shelled

- 1 tablespoon flax seed

- 2 tablespoons pecans, chopped

- 2 tablespoons hazelnuts, chopped

- 2 tablespoons almonds, chopped

- 2 tablespoons walnuts, chopped

- ½ teaspoon ground cinnamon

- 1/8 t teaspoon ground cloves

Instructions:

1. In a small bowl, add the oil and maple syrup and mix well.

2. In a large bowl, add the remaining ingredients and mix well.

3. Add the oil mixture and mix until well combined.

4. Place the mixture into a baking dish.

5. Select "Air Fry" of Breville Smart Air Fryer Oven and adjust the temperature to 350 degrees F.

6. Set the timer for 15 minutes and press "Start/Stop" to begin preheating.

7. When the unit beeps to show that it is preheated, arrange the baking dish over the wire rack.

8. While cooking, stir the granola after every 5 minutes.

9. When the cooking time is complete, remove the baking dish from the oven.

10. Set the granola aside to cool completely before serving.

Dried Fruit Oatmeal

Servings: 8

Preparation Time: 10 minutes

Cooking Time: 8 hours

Ingredients:

- 2 cups steel-cut oats

- 1/3 cup dried apricots, chopped

- 1/3 cup raisins

- 1/3 cup dried cherries

- 1 teaspoon ground cinnamon

- 6 cups water

- 4 cups milk

- 4 cups water

- ¼ teaspoon liquid stevia

Instructions:

1. In an oven-safe pan that will fit in the Breville Smart Air Fryer Oven, place all ingredients and stir to combine.

2. Cover the pan with a lid.

3. Arrange the pan over the wire rack.

4. Select "Slow Cooker" of Breville Smart Air Fryer Oven and set on "Low".

5. Set the timer for 8 hours and press "Start/Stop" to begin cooking.

6. When the cooking time is complete, remove the pan from the oven.

7. Remove the lid and stir the mixture well.

8. Serve warm.

Cinnamon French Toasts

Servings: 2

Preparation Time: 10 minutes

Cooking Time: 5 minutes

Ingredients:

- 2 eggs

- ¼ cup whole milk

- 3 tablespoons sugar

- 2 teaspoons olive oil

- 1/8 teaspoon vanilla extract

- 1/8 teaspoon ground cinnamon

- 4 bread slices

Instructions:

1. In a large bowl, add all the ingredients except for bread slices and beat until well combined.

2. Coat the bread slices with egg mixture evenly.

3. Arrange the bread slices in the air fry basket.

4. Select "Air Fry" of Breville Smart Air Fryer Oven and adjust the temperature to 390 degrees F.

5. Set the timer for 5 minutes and press "Start/Stop" to begin preheating.

6. When the unit beeps to show that it is preheated, insert the air fry basket in the oven.

7. Flip the bread slices once halfway through.

8. When the cooking time is complete, remove the air fry basket from the oven.

9. Serve warm.

Cheddar Mustard Toasts

Servings: 2

Preparation Time: 10 minutes

Cooking Time: 10 minutes

Ingredients:

- 4 bread slices

- 2 tablespoons cheddar cheese, shredded

- 2 eggs, whites and yolks, separated

- 1 tablespoon mustard

- 1 tablespoon paprika

Instructions:

1. In a clean glass bowl, add the egg whites in and beat until they form soft peaks.

2. In another bowl, mix together the cheese, egg yolks, mustard, and paprika.

3. Gently fold in the egg whites.

4. Spread the mustard mixture over the toasted bread slices.

5. Arrange the bread slices in the air fry basket.

6. Select "Air Fry" of Breville Smart Air Fryer Oven and adjust the temperature to 355 degrees F.

7. Set the timer for 10 minutes and press "Start/Stop" to begin preheating.

8. When the unit beeps to show that it is preheated, insert the air fry basket in the oven.

9. When the cooking time is complete, remove the air fry basket from the oven.

10. Serve warm.

Cheese Toasts with Bacon

Servings: 2

Preparation Time: 10 minutes

Cooking Time: 4 minutes

Ingredients:

- 4 bread slices

- 1 garlic clove, minced

- 4 ounces goat cheese, crumbled

- Freshly ground black pepper, to taste

- 8 cooked bacon slices, crumbled

Instructions:

1. In a food processor, add the garlic, ricotta, lemon zest and black pepper and pulse until smooth.

2. Spread ricotta mixture over each bread slices evenly.

3. Arrange the bread slices in the air fry basket.

4. Select "Air Fry" of Breville Smart Air Fryer Oven and adjust the temperature to 355 degrees F.

5. Set the timer for 4 minutes and press "Start/Stop" to begin preheating.

6. When the unit beeps to show that it is preheated, insert the air fry basket in the oven.

7. When the cooking time is complete, remove the air fry basket from the oven and transfer the bread slices onto serving plates.

8. Top with bacon pieces and serve.

Parmesan Eggs in Avocado Cups

Servings: 2

Preparation Time: 10 minutes

Cooking Time: 12 minutes

Ingredients:

- 1 avocado, halved and pitted

- Salt and ground black pepper, as required

- 2 eggs

- 1 tablespoon Parmesan cheese, shredded

Instructions:

1. Arrange a greased square piece of foil in the air fry basket.

2. Select "Bake" of Breville Smart Air Fryer Oven and adjust the temperature to 390 degrees F.

3. Set the timer for 12 minutes and press "Start/Stop" to begin preheating.

4. Meanwhile, carefully scoop out about 2 teaspoons of flesh from each avocado half.

5. Crack 1 egg in each avocado half and sprinkle with salt, black pepper and cheese.

9. When the unit beeps to show that it is preheated, arrange the avocado halves into the prepared air fry basket and insert in the oven.

10. When the cooking time is complete, transfer the avocado halves onto serving plates.

11. Top with Parmesan and serve.

Eggs in Bread Cups

Servings: 4

Preparation Time: 10 minutes

Cooking Time: 23 minutes

Ingredients:

- 4 bacon slices

- 2 bread slices, crust removed

- 4 eggs

- Salt and ground black pepper, as required

Instructions:

1. Grease 4 cups of the muffin tin and set aside.

2. Heat a small frying pan over medium-high heat and cook the bacon slices for about 2-3 minutes.

3. With a slotted spoon, transfer the bacon slice onto a paper towel-lined plate to cool.

4. Break each bread slice in half.

5. Arrange 1 bread slice half in each of the prepared muffin cups and press slightly.

6. Now, arrange 1 bacon slice over each bread slice in a circular shape.

7. Crack 1 egg into each muffin cup and sprinkle with salt and black pepper.

8. Select "Bake" of Breville Smart Air Fryer Oven and adjust the temperature to 350 degrees F.

9. Set the timer for 20 minutes and press "Start/Stop" to begin preheating.

10. When the unit beeps to show that it is preheated, arrange the muffin tin over the wire rack.

11. When the cooking time is complete, remove the muffin tin from the oven.

12. Serve warm.

Eggs in Bread & Bacon Cups

Servings: 4

Preparation Time: 10 minutes

Cooking Time: 15 minutes

Ingredients:

- 4 bacon slices

- 4 bread slices

- 1 scallion, chopped

- 2 tablespoons bell pepper, seeded and chopped

- 1½ tablespoons mayonnaise

- 4 eggs

Instructions:

1. Grease 6 cups of the muffin tin.

2. Line the sides of each prepared muffin cup with 1 bacon slice.

3. Cut bread slices with a round cookie cutter.

4. Arrange the bread slice in the bottom of each muffin cup.

5. Top with scallion, bell pepper and mayonnaise evenly.

6. Carefully crack one egg in each muffin cup.

7. Select "Air Fry" of Breville Smart Air Fryer Oven and adjust the temperature to 375 degrees F.

8. Set the timer for 15 minutes and press "Start/Stop" to begin preheating.

9. When the unit beeps to show that it is preheated, arrange the muffin tin over the wire rack.

10. When the cooking time is complete, remove the muffin tin from the oven.

11. Serve warm.

Baked Eggs

Servings: 4

Preparation Time: 10 minutes

Cooking Time: 12 minutes

Ingredients:

- 1 cup marinara sauce, divided

- 1 tablespoon capers, drained and divided

- 8 eggs

- ¼ cup whipping cream, divided

- ¼ cup Parmesan cheese, shredded and divided

- Salt and ground black pepper, as required

Instructions:

1. Grease 4 ramekins. Set aside.

2. Divide the marinara sauce in the bottom of each prepared ramekin evenly and top with capers.

3. Carefully crack 2 eggs over marinara sauce into each ramekin and top with cream, followed by the Parmesan cheese.

4. Sprinkle each ramekin with salt and black pepper.

5. Select "Bake" of Breville Smart Air Fryer Oven and adjust the temperature to 400 degrees F.

6. Set the timer for 12 minutes and press "Start/Stop" to begin preheating.

7. When the unit beeps to show that it is preheated, arrange the ramekins over the wire rack.

8. When the cooking time is complete, remove the ramekins from the oven.

9. Serve warm.

Egg & Spinach Tart

Servings: 4

Preparation Time: 15 minutes

Cooking Time: 25 minutes

Ingredients:

- 1 puff pastry sheet, trimmed into a 9x13-inch rectangle

- 4 eggs

- ½ cup cheddar cheese, grated

- 7 cooked thick-cut bacon strips

- ½ cup cooked spinach

- 1 egg, lightly beaten

Instructions:

1. Arrange the pastry in a lightly greased enamel roasting pan.

2. With a small knife gently, cut a 1-inch border around the edges of the puff pastry without cutting all the way through.

3. With a fork, pierce the center of the pastry a few times.

4. Select "Bake" of Breville Smart Air Fryer Oven and adjust the temperature to 400 degrees F.

5. Set the timer for 10 minutes and press "Start/Stop" to begin preheating.

6. When the unit beeps to show that it is preheated, insert the roasting pan in the oven.

7. When the cooking time is complete, remove the roasting pan from the oven and sprinkle the cheese over the center.

8. Place the spinach and bacon in an even layer across the tart.

9. Now, crack the eggs, leaving space between each one.

10. Select "Bake" of Breville Smart Air Fryer Oven and adjust the temperature to 400 degrees F.

11. Set the timer for 15 minutes and press "Start/Stop" to begin preheating.

12. Insert the roasting pan in the oven.

13. When the cooking time is complete, remove the roasting pan from the oven and set aside to cool for 2-3 minutes before cutting.

14. With a pizza cutter, cut into 4 portions and serve.

Cheddar & Cream Omelet

Servings: 2

Preparation Time: 10 minutes

Cooking Time: 8 minutes

Ingredients:

- 4 eggs

- ¼ cup cream

- Salt and ground black pepper, as required

- ¼ cup Cheddar cheese, grated

Instructions:

1. In a bowl, add the eggs, cream, salt, and black pepper and beat well.

2. Place the egg mixture into a small baking dish.

3. Select "Air Fry" of Breville Smart Air Fryer Oven and adjust the temperature to 350 degrees F.

4. Set the timer for 8 minutes and press "Start/Stop" to begin preheating.

5. When the unit beeps to show that it is preheated, arrange the baking dish over the wire rack.

6. After 4 minutes of cooking, sprinkle the omelet with cheese evenly.

7. When the cooking time is complete, remove the baking dish from oven.

8. Cut the omelet into 2 portions and serve hot.

Bell Pepper Omelet

Servings: 2

Preparation Time: 10 minutes

Cooking Time: 10 minutes

Ingredients:

- 1 teaspoon butter

- 1 small onion, sliced

- ½ of green bell pepper, seeded and chopped

- 4 eggs

- ¼ teaspoon milk

- Salt and ground black pepper, as required

- ¼ cup Cheddar cheese, grated

Instructions:

1. In a skillet, melt the butter over medium heat and cook the onion and bell pepper for about 4-5 minutes.

2. Remove the skillet from heat and set aside to cool slightly.

3. Meanwhile, in a bowl, add the eggs, milk, salt and black pepper and beat well.

4. Add the cooked onion mixture and gently stir to combine.

5. Place the bell pepper mixture into a small baking dish.

6. Select "Air Fry" of Breville Smart Air Fryer Oven and adjust the temperature to 355 degrees F.

7. Set the timer for 10 minutes and press "Start/Stop" to begin preheating.

8. When the unit beeps to show that it is preheated, arrange the baking dish over the wire rack.

9. When the cooking time is complete, remove the baking dish from oven and place onto a wire rack to cool for about 5 minutes before serving.

10. Cut the omelet into 2 portions and serve hot.

Turkey & Zucchini Omelet

Servings: 6

Preparation Time: 15 minutes

Cooking Time: 35 minutes

Ingredients:

- 8 eggs

- ½ cup unsweetened almond milk

- 1/8 teaspoon red pepper flakes, crushed

- Salt and ground black pepper, as required

- 1 cup cooked turkey meat, chopped

- 1 cup Monterrey Jack cheese, shredded

- ½ cup fresh scallion, chopped

- ¾ cup zucchini, chopped

Instructions:

1. In a bowl, add the eggs, almond milk, salt and black pepper and beat well.

2. Add the remaining ingredients and stir to combine.

3. Place the mixture into a greased baking dish.

4. Select "Bake" of Breville Smart Air Fryer Oven and adjust the temperature to 315 degrees F.

5. Set the timer for 35 minutes and press "Start/Stop" to begin preheating.

6. When the unit beeps to show that it is preheated, arrange the baking dish over the wire rack.

7. When the cooking time is complete, remove the baking dish from the oven and place onto a wire rack to cool for about 5 minutes before serving.

8. Cut into equal-sized wedges and serve.

Pepperoni Omelet

Servings: 2

Preparation Time: 15 minutes

Cooking Time: 12 minutes

Ingredients:

- 4 eggs

- 2 tablespoons milk

- Pinch of salt

- Ground black pepper, as required

- 8-10 turkey pepperoni slices

Instructions:

1. In a bowl, crack the eggs and beat well.

2. Add the remaining ingredients and gently stir to combine.

3. Place the mixture into a baking dish.

4. Select "Air Fry" of Breville Smart Air Fryer Oven and adjust the temperature to 355 degrees F.

5. Set the timer for 12 minutes and press "Start/Stop" to begin preheating.

6. When the unit beeps to show that it is preheated, arrange the baking dish over the wire rack.

7. When the cooking time is complete, remove the baking dish from oven.

8. Cut into equal-sized wedges and serve.

Egg & Tofu Omelet

Servings: 2

Preparation Time: 15 minutes

Cooking Time: 10 minutes

Ingredients:

- 1 teaspoon arrowroot starch

- 2 teaspoons water

- 3 eggs

- 2 teaspoons fish sauce

- 1 teaspoon olive oil

- Ground black pepper, as required

- 8 ounces silken tofu, pressed and sliced

Instructions:

1. In a large bowl, dissolve arrowroot starch in water.

2. Add the eggs, fish sauce, oil and black pepper and beat well.

3. Place tofu in the bottom of a greased baking dish and top with the egg mixture.

4. Select "Air Fry" of Breville Smart Air Fryer Oven and adjust the temperature to 390 degrees F.

5. Set the timer for 10 minutes and press "Start/Stop" to begin preheating.

6. When the unit beeps to show that it is preheated, arrange the baking dish over the wire rack.

7. When the cooking time is complete, remove the baking dish from oven and place onto a wire rack to cool for about 5 minutes before serving.

8. Cut into equal-sized wedges and serve.

Mini Veggie Frittatas

Servings: 2

Preparation Time: 15 minutes

Cooking Time: 17 minutes

Ingredients:

- 1 tablespoon butter

- ½ of white onion, sliced thinly

- 1 cup fresh mushrooms, sliced thinly

- 1 ¼ cups fresh spinach, chopped

- 3 eggs

- ½ teaspoon fresh rosemary, chopped

- Salt and ground black pepper, as required

- 3 tablespoons Parmesan cheese, shredded

Instructions:

1. In a frying pan, melt butter over medium heat and cook the onion and mushroom for about 3 minutes.

2. Add the spinach and cook for about 2-3 minutes.

3. Remove the frying pan from heat and set aside to cool slightly.

4. Meanwhile, in a small bowl, add the eggs, rosemary, salt and black pepper and beat well.

5. Divide the beaten eggs in 2 greased ramekins evenly and top with the veggie mixture, followed by the cheese.

6. Select "Air Fry" of Breville Smart Air Fryer Oven and adjust the temperature to 330 degrees F.

7. Set the timer for 12 minutes and press "Start/Stop" to begin preheating.

8. When the unit beeps to show that it is preheated, place the ramekins over the air rack.

9. When the cooking time is complete, remove the ramekins from the oven and place onto a wire rack for about 5 minutes before serving.

Spinach & Tomato Frittata

Servings: 6

Preparation Time: 15 minutes

Cooking Time: 30 minutes

Ingredients:

- 10 large eggs

- Salt and ground black pepper, as required

- 1 (5-ounce) bag baby spinach

- 2 cups grape tomatoes, halved

- 4 scallions, sliced thinly

- 8 ounces feta cheese, crumbled

- 3 tablespoons hot olive oil

Instructions:

1. In a bowl, place the eggs, salt and black pepper and beat well.

2. Add the spinach, tomatoes, scallions and feta cheese and gently stir to combine.

3. Spread the oil in a baking dish and top with the spinach mixture.

4. Select "Bake" of Breville Smart Air Fryer Oven and adjust the temperature to 350 degrees F.

5. Set the timer for 30 minutes and press "Start/Stop" to begin preheating.

6. When the unit beeps to show that it is preheated, arrange the baking dish over the wire rack.

7. When the cooking time is complete, remove the baking dish from oven and place onto a wire rack to cool for about 5 minutes before serving.

8. Cut into equal-sized wedges and serve.

Beef Frittata

Servings: 4

Preparation Time: 15 minutes

Cooking Time: 20 minutes

Ingredients:

- ½ pound cooked ground beef, grease removed

- 1 cup Colby Jack cheese, shredded

- 8 eggs, beaten lightly

- 4 scallions, chopped

- 1/8 teaspoon red pepper flakes, crushed

- Salt and ground black pepper, as required

Instructions:

1. In a bowl, add the sausage, cheese, eggs, scallion and cayenne and mix until well combined.

2. Place the mixture into a greased baking dish.

3. Select "Air Fry" of Breville Smart Air Fryer Oven and adjust the temperature to 360 degrees F.

4. Set the timer for 20 minutes and press "Start/Stop" to begin preheating.

5. When the unit beeps to show that it is preheated, arrange the baking dish over the wire rack.

6. When the cooking time is complete, remove the baking dish from oven and place onto a wire rack to cool for about 5 minutes before serving.

7. Cut into 4 wedges and serve.

Trout Frittata

Servings: 4

Preparation Time: 15 minutes

Cooking Time: 25 minutes

Ingredients:

- 1 tablespoon olive oil

- 1 onion, sliced

- 6 eggs

- ½ tablespoon horseradish sauce

- 2 tablespoons crème fraiche

- 2 hot-smoked trout fillets, chopped

- ¼ cup fresh dill, chopped

Instructions:

1. In a skillet, heat the oil over medium heat and cook the onion for about 4-5 minutes.

2. Remove from the heat and set aside.

3. Meanwhile, in a bowl, add the eggs, horseradish sauce, and crème fraiche and mix well.

4. In the bottom of a baking dish, place the cooked onion and top with the egg mixture, followed by trout.

5. Select "Air Fry" of Breville Smart Air Fryer Oven and adjust the temperature to 320 degrees F.

6. Set the timer for 20 minutes and press "Start/Stop" to begin preheating.

7. When the unit beeps to show that it is preheated, arrange the baking dish over the wire rack.

8. When the cooking time is complete, remove the baking dish from oven and place onto a wire rack to cool for about 5 minutes before serving.

9. Cut into equal-sized wedges and serve with the garnishing of dill.

Tomato Quiche

Servings: 2

Preparation Time: 15 minutes

Cooking Time: 30 minutes

Ingredients:

- 4 eggs

- ¼ cup onion, chopped

- ½ cup tomatoes, chopped

- ½ cup milk

- 1 cup Gouda cheese, shredded

- Salt, as required

Instructions:

1. In a small baking dish, add all the ingredients and mix well.

2. Select "Air Fry" of Breville Smart Air Fryer Oven and adjust the temperature to 340 degrees F.

3. Set the timer for 30 minutes and press "Start/Stop" to begin preheating.

4. When the unit beeps to show that it is preheated, arrange the baking dish over the wire rack.

5. When the cooking time is complete, remove the baking dish from oven and place onto a wire rack to cool for about 5 minutes before serving.

6. Cut into equal-sized wedges and serve.

Chicken & Broccoli Quiche

Servings: 2

Preparation Time: 15 minutes

Cooking Time: 12 minutes

Ingredients:

- ½ of frozen ready-made pie crust

- ¼ tablespoon olive oil

- 1 small egg

- 3 tablespoons cheddar cheese, grated

- 1 ½ tablespoons whipping cream

- Salt and freshly ground black pepper, as needed

- 3 tablespoons boiled broccoli, chopped

- 2 tablespoons cooked chicken, chopped

Instructions:

1. Cut 1 (5-inch) round from the pie crust.

2. Arrange the pie crust round in a small pie pan and gently press in the bottom and sides.

3. In a bowl, mix together the egg, cheese, cream, salt, and black pepper.

4. Pour the egg mixture over the dough base and top with the broccoli and chicken.

5. Select "Air Fry" of Breville Smart Air Fryer Oven and adjust the temperature to 390 degrees F.

6. Set the timer for 12 minutes and press "Start/Stop" to begin preheating.

7. When the unit beeps to show that it is preheated, arrange the pie pan over the wire rack.

8. When the cooking time is complete, remove the pie pan from oven and place onto a wire rack to cool for about 5 minutes before serving.

9. Cut into equal-sized wedges and serve.

Bacon & Spinach Quiche

Servings: 4

Preparation Time: 15 minutes

Cooking Time: 12 minutes

Ingredients:

- 2 cooked bacon slices, chopped

- ½ cup fresh spinach, chopped

- ¼ cup mozzarella cheese, shredded

- ½ cup Parmesan cheese, shredded

- 2 tablespoons milk

- 2 dashes Tabasco sauce

- Salt and ground black pepper, as required

Instructions:

1. In a bowl, add all ingredients and mix well.

2. Transfer the mixture into a baking dish.

3. Select "Air Fry" of Breville Smart Air Fryer Oven and adjust the temperature to 320 degrees F.

4. Set the timer for 12 minutes and press "Start/Stop" to begin preheating.

5. When the unit beeps to show that it is preheated, arrange the baking dish over the wire rack.

6. When the cooking time is complete, remove the baking dish from oven and place onto a wire rack to cool for about 5 minutes before serving.

7. Cut into equal-sized wedges and serve hot.

Salmon Quiche

Servings: 2

Preparation Time: 15 minutes

Cooking Time: 20 minutes

Ingredients:

- 5½ ounces salmon fillet, chopped

- Salt and ground black pepper, as required

- ½ tablespoon fresh lemon juice

- 1 egg yolk

- 3½ tablespoons chilled butter

- 2/3 cup flour

- 1 tablespoon cold water

- 2 eggs

- 3 tablespoons whipping cream

- 1 scallion, chopped

Instructions:

1. In a bowl, add the salmon, salt, black pepper and lemon juice and mix well.

2. In another bowl, add the egg yolk, butter, flour and water and mix until a dough forms.

3. Place the dough onto a floured smooth surface and roll into about 7-inch round.

4. Place the dough in a quiche pan and press firmly in the bottom and along the edges.

5. Trim the excess edges.

6. In a small bowl, add the eggs, cream, salt and black pepper and beat until well combined.

7. Place the cream mixture over the crust evenly and top with the salmon mixture, followed by the scallion.

8. Select "Air Fry" of Breville Smart Air Fryer Oven and adjust the temperature to 355 degrees F.

9. Set the timer for 20 minutes and press "Start/Stop" to begin preheating.

10. When the unit beeps to show that it is preheated, arrange the quiche pan over the wire rack.

11. When the cooking time is complete, remove the quiche pan from the oven and set aside for about 5 minutes before serving.

12. Cut the quiche into equal-sized wedges and serve

Sausage & Mushroom Casserole

Servings: 6
Preparation Time: 15 minutes
Cooking Time: 19 minutes

Ingredients:

- 1 tablespoon olive oil

- ½ pound spicy ground sausage

- ¾ cup yellow onion, chopped

- 5 fresh mushrooms, sliced

- 8 eggs, beaten

- ½ teaspoon garlic salt

- ¾ cup Cheddar cheese, shredded and divided

- ¼ cup Alfredo sauce

Instructions:

1. In a skillet, heat the oil over medium heat and cook the sausage and onions for about 4-5 minutes.

2. Add the mushrooms and cook for about 6-7 minutes.

3. Remove from the oven and drain the grease from the skillet.

4. In a bowl, add the sausage mixture, beaten eggs, garlic salt, ½ cup of cheese and Alfredo sauce and stir to combine.

5. Place the sausage mixture into a baking dish.

6. Select "Air Fry" of Breville Smart Air Fryer Oven and adjust the temperature to 390 degrees F.

7. Set the timer for 12 minutes and press "Start/Stop" to begin preheating.

8. When the unit beeps to show that it is preheated, arrange the baking dish over the wire rack.

9. After 6 minutes of cooking, stir the sausage mixture well.

10. When the cooking time is complete, remove the baking dish from oven and place onto a wire rack to cool for about 5 minutes before serving.

11. Cut into equal-sized wedges and serve with the topping of remaining cheese.

Ham & Hashbrown Casserole

Servings: 5

Preparation Time: 15 minutes

Cooking Time: 35 minutes

Ingredients:

- 1 ½ tablespoons olive oil

- ½ of large onion, chopped

- 24 ounces frozen Hashbrown

- 3 eggs

- 2 tablespoons milk

- Salt and ground black pepper, as required

- ½ pound ham, chopped

- ¼ cup Cheddar cheese, shredded

Instructions:

1. In a skillet, heat the oil over medium heat and sauté the onion for about 4-5 minutes.

2. Remove from the heat and transfer the onion into a bowl.

3. Add the hashbrowns and mix well.

4. Place the mixture into a baking dish.

5. Select "Bake" of Breville Smart Air Fryer Oven and adjust the temperature to 350 degrees F.

6. Set the timer for 32 minutes and press "Start/Stop" to begin preheating.

7. When the unit beeps to show that it is preheated, arrange the baking dish over the wire rack.

8. Stir the mixture once after 8 minutes.

9. Meanwhile, in a bowl, add the eggs, milk, salt and black pepper and beat well.

10. After 15 minutes of cooking, place the egg mixture over hashbrown mixture evenly and top with the ham.

11. After 30 minutes of cooking, sprinkle the casserole with the cheese.

12. When the cooking time is complete, remove the baking dish from oven and place onto a wire rack to cool for about 5 minutes before serving.

13. Cut into equal-sized wedges and serve.

Eggs with Turkey & Spinach

Servings: 4

Preparation Time: 15 minutes

Cooking Time: 23 minutes

Ingredients:

- 1 tablespoon unsalted butter

- 1 pound fresh baby spinach

- 4 eggs

- 7 ounces cooked turkey, chopped

- 4 teaspoons milk

- Salt and ground black pepper, as required

Instructions:

1. In a skillet, melt the butter over medium heat and cook the spinach for about 2-3 minutes or until just wilted.

2. Remove from the heat and transfer the spinach into a bowl.

3. Set aside to cool slightly.

4. Divide the spinach into 4 greased ramekins, followed by the turkey.

5. Crack 1 egg into each ramekin and drizzle with milk.

6. Sprinkle with salt and black pepper.

7. Select "Air Fry" of Breville Smart Air Fryer Oven and adjust the temperature to 355 degrees F.

8. Set the timer for 20 minutes and press "Start/Stop" to begin preheating.

9. When the unit beeps to show that it is preheated, arrange the ramekins over the wire rack.

10. When the cooking time is complete, remove the ramekins from oven and place onto a wire rack to cool for about 5 minutes before serving.

Eggs with Ham

Servings: 2

Preparation Time: 10 minutes

Cooking Time: 13 minutes

Ingredients:

- 2 teaspoons unsalted butter, softened

- 2 ounces ham, sliced thinly

- 4 large eggs, divided

- Salt and ground black pepper, as required

- 2 tablespoons heavy cream

- 1/8 teaspoon smoked paprika

- 3 tablespoons Parmesan cheese, grated finely

- 2 teaspoons fresh chives, minced

Instructions:

1. In the bottom of a baking dish, spread the butter.

2. Arrange the ham slices over the butter.

3. In a bowl, add 1 egg, salt, black pepper and cream and beat until smooth.

4. Place the egg mixture over the ham slices evenly.

5. Carefully crack the remaining eggs on top and sprinkle with paprika, salt, black pepper, cheese and chives evenly.

6. Select "Air Fry" of Breville Smart Air Fryer Oven and adjust the temperature to 320 degrees F.

7. Set the timer for 13 minutes and press "Start/Stop" to begin preheating.

8. When the unit beeps to show that it is preheated, arrange the baking dish over the wire rack.

9. When the cooking time is complete, remove the baking dish from the oven and set aside for about 5 minutes before serving.

10. Cut into equal-sized wedges and serve.

Cranberry Muffins

Servings: 8

Preparation Time: 25 minutes

Cooking Time: 15 minutes

Ingredients:

- ¼ cup unsweetened almond milk

- 2 large eggs

- ½ teaspoon vanilla extract

- 1 ½ cups almond flour

- ¼ cup Erythritol

- 1 teaspoon baking powder

- ¼ teaspoon ground cinnamon

- 1/8 teaspoon salt

- ½ cup fresh cranberries

- ¼ cup walnuts, chopped

Instructions:

1. In a blender, add the almond milk, eggs and vanilla extract and pulse for about 20-30 seconds.

2. Add the almond flour, Erythritol, baking powder, cinnamon and salt and pulse for about 30-45 seconds until well blended.

3. Transfer the mixture into a bowl.

4. Gently fold in half of the cranberries and walnuts.

5. Place the mixture into 8 silicone muffin cups and top each with remaining cranberries.

6. Select "Air Fry" of Breville Smart Air Fryer Oven and adjust the temperature to 325 degrees F.

7. Set the timer for 15 minutes and press "Start/Stop" to begin preheating.

8. When the unit beeps to show that it is preheated, arrange the muffin cups over the wire rack.

9. When the cooking time is complete, remove the muffin cups from oven and place onto a wire rack to cool for about 10 minutes.

10. Carefully invert the muffins onto the wire rack to completely cool before serving.

Blueberry Muffins

Servings: 12
Preparation Time: 16 minutes
Cooking Time: 12 minutes

Ingredients:

- 2 cups plus 2 tablespoons self-rising flour

- 5 tablespoons white sugar

- ½ cup milk

- 2 ounces butter, melted

- 2 eggs

- 2 teaspoons fresh orange zest, finely grated

- 2 tablespoons fresh orange juice

- ½ teaspoon vanilla extract

- ½ cup fresh blueberries

Instructions:

1. Grease 12 cups of the muffin tin. Set aside.

2. In a bowl, mix together the flour and white sugar.

3. In another large bowl, mix well the remaining ingredients except for blueberries.

4. Add the flour mixture and mix until just combined.

5. Fold in the blueberries.

6. Place the mixture into the prepared muffin cups.

7. Select "Air Fry" of Breville Smart Air Fryer Oven and adjust the temperature to 355 degrees F.

8. Set the timer for 12 minutes and press "Start/Stop" to begin preheating.

9. When the unit beeps to show that it is preheated, arrange the muffin tin over the wire rack.

10. When the cooking time is complete, remove the muffin tin from oven and place onto a wire rack to cool for about 10 minutes.

11. Carefully invert the muffins onto the wire rack to completely cool before serving.

Savory Carrot Muffins

Servings: 6

Preparation Time: 15 minutes

Cooking Time: 7 minutes

Ingredients:

For Muffins:

- ¼ cup whole-wheat flour

- ¼ cup all-purpose flour

- ½ teaspoon baking powder

- 1/8 teaspoon baking soda

- ½ teaspoon dried parsley, crushed

- ½ teaspoon salt

- ½ cup plain yogurt

- 1 teaspoon vinegar

- 1 tablespoon vegetable oil

- 3 tablespoons cottage cheese, grated

- 1 carrot, peeled and grated

- 2-4 tablespoons water (if needed)

For Topping:

- 7 ounces Parmesan cheese, grated

- ¼ cup walnuts, chopped

Instructions:

1. For muffins: in a large bowl, mix together the flours, baking powder, baking soda, parsley, and salt.

2. In another large bowl, add the yogurt and vinegar and mix well.

3. Add the remaining ingredients except for water and beat them well. (Add some water if needed).

4. Make a well in the center of the yogurt mixture.

5. Slowly add the flour mixture in the well and mix until well combined.

6. Place the mixture into lightly greased 6 medium-sized muffin molds evenly and top with the Parmesan cheese and walnuts.

7. Select "Air Fry" of Breville Smart Air Fryer Oven and adjust the temperature to 355 degrees F.

8. Set the timer for 7 minutes and press "Start/Stop" to begin preheating.

9. When the unit beeps to show that it is preheated, arrange the muffin molds over the wire rack.

10. When the cooking time is complete, remove the muffin molds from the oven and place onto a wire rack to cool for about 5 minutes.

11. Carefully invert the muffins onto the platter and serve warm.

Bacon & Spinach Muffins

Servings: 6

Preparation Time: 10 minutes

Cooking Time: 17 minutes

Ingredients:

- 6 eggs

- ½ cup milk

- Salt and ground black pepper, as required

- 1 cup fresh spinach, chopped

- 4 cooked bacon slices, crumbled

Instructions:

1. In a bowl, add the eggs, milk, salt and black pepper and beat until well combined.

2. Add the spinach and stir to combine.

3. Divide the spinach mixture into 6 greased cups of an egg bite mold evenly.

4. Select "Air Fry" of Breville Smart Air Fryer Oven and adjust the temperature to 325 degrees F.

5. Set the timer for 17 minutes and press "Start/Stop" to begin preheating.

6. When the unit beeps to show that it is preheated, arrange the egg bite mold over the wire rack.

7. When the cooking time is complete, remove the egg bite mold from oven and place onto a wire rack to cool for about 5 minutes.

8. Top with bacon pieces and serve warm.

Ham Muffins

Servings: 6

Preparation Time: q0 minutes

Cooking Time: 18 minutes

Ingredients:

- 6 ham slices

- 6 eggs

- 6 tablespoons cream

- 3 tablespoon mozzarella cheese, shredded

- ¼ teaspoon dried basil, crushed

Instructions:

1. Lightly grease 6 cups of the muffin tin.

2. Line each prepared muffin cup with 1 ham slice.

3. Crack 1 egg into each muffin cup and top with cream.

4. Sprinkle with cheese and basil.

5. Select "Air Fry" of Breville Smart Air Fryer Oven and adjust the temperature to 350 degrees F.

6. Set the timer for 18 minutes and press "Start/Stop" to begin preheating.

7. When the unit beeps to show that it is preheated, arrange the muffin tin over the wire rack.

8. When the cooking time is complete, remove the muffin tin from oven and place onto a wire rack to cool for about 10 minutes.

9. Carefully invert the muffins onto the platter and serve warm.

Yogurt Bread

Servings: 10

Preparation Time: 20 minutes

Cooking Time: 40 minutes

Ingredients:

- 1½ cups warm water, divided

- 1½ teaspoons active dry yeast

- 1 teaspoon sugar

- 3 cups all-purpose flour

- 1 cup plain Greek yogurt

- 2 teaspoons kosher salt

Instructions:

1. In the bowl of a stand mixer, fitted with the dough hook attachment, add ½ cup of the warm water, yeast and sugar and mix well.

2. Set aside for about 5 minutes.

3. Add the flour, yogurt, and salt and mix on medium-low speed until the dough comes together.

4. Then, mix on medium speed for 5 minutes.

5. Place the dough into a bowl.

6. With a plastic wrap, cover the bowl and place in a warm place for about 2-3 hours or until doubled in size.

7. Transfer the dough onto a lightly floured surface and shape into a smooth ball.

8. Place the dough onto a greased parchment paper-lined rack.

9. With a kitchen towel, cover the dough and let rest for 15 minutes.

10. With a very sharp knife, cut a 4x½-inch deep cut down the center of the dough.

11. Select "Roast" of Breville Smart Air Fryer Oven and adjust the temperature to 325 degrees F.

12. Set the timer for 40 minutes and press "Start/Stop" to begin preheating.

13. When the unit beeps to show that it is preheated, arrange the dough over the wire rack.

14. When the cooking time is complete, remove the bread from the oven and place onto a wire rack to cool completely before slicing.

15. Cut the bread into desired-sized slices and serve.

Date Bread

Servings: 10

Preparation Time: 15 minutes

Cooking Time: 22 minutes

Ingredients:

- 2½ cup dates, pitted and chopped

- ¼ cup butter

- 1 cup hot water

- 1½ cups flour

- ½ cup brown sugar

- 1 teaspoon baking powder

- 1 teaspoon baking soda

- ½ teaspoon salt

- 1 egg

Instructions:

1. In a large bowl, add the dates, butter and top with the hot water. Set aside for about 5 minutes.

2. In another bowl, mix together the flour, brown sugar, baking powder, baking soda, and salt.

3. In the same bowl of dates, add the flour mixture and egg and mix well.

4. Grease a baking dish.

5. Place the mixture into the prepared baking dish.

6. Select "Air Fry" of Breville Smart Air Fryer Oven and adjust the temperature to 340 degrees F.

7. Set the timer for 22 minutes and press "Start/Stop" to begin preheating.

8. When the unit beeps to show that it is preheated, arrange the baking dish over the wire rack.

9. When the cooking time is complete, remove the baking dish from oven and place onto a wire rack to cool for about 10 minutes.

10. Carefully invert the bread onto the wire rack to cool completely before slicing.

11. Cut the bread into desired-sized slices and serve.

Banana & Walnut Bread

Servings: 10

Preparation Time: 15 minutes

Cooking Time: 25 minutes

Ingredients:

- 1½ cups self-rising flour

- ¼ teaspoon bicarbonate of soda

- 5 tablespoons plus 1 teaspoon butter

- 2/3 cup plus ½ tablespoon caster sugar

- 2 medium eggs

- 3½ ounces walnuts, chopped

- 2 cups bananas, peeled and mashed

Instructions:

1. In a bowl, mix together the flour and bicarbonate of soda.

2. In another bowl, add the butter and sugar and beat until pale and fluffy.

3. Add the eggs, one at a time along with a little flour and mix well.

4. Stir in the remaining flour and walnuts.

5. Add the bananas and mix until well combined.

6. Grease a loaf pan.

7. Place the mixture into the prepared pan.

8. Select "Air Fry" of Breville Smart Air Fryer Oven and adjust the temperature to 355 degrees F.

9. Set the timer for 10 minutes and press "Start/Stop" to begin preheating.

10. When the unit beeps to show that it is preheated, arrange the loaf pan over the wire rack.

11. After 10 minutes of cooking, set the temperature at 338 degrees F for 15 minutes.

12. When the cooking time is complete, remove the loaf pan from oven and place onto a wire rack to cool for about 10 minutes.

13. Carefully invert the bread onto the wire rack to cool completely before slicing.

14. Cut the bread into desired-sized slices and serve.

Zucchini & Apple Bread

Servings: 8

Preparation Time: 15 minutes

Cooking Time: 30 minutes

Ingredients:

For Bread:

- 1 cup all-purpose flour

- ¾ teaspoon baking powder

- ¼ teaspoon baking soda

- 1¼ teaspoons ground cinnamon

- ¼ teaspoon salt

- 1/3 cup vegetable oil

- 1/3 cup sugar

- 1 egg

- 1 teaspoon vanilla extract

- ½ cup zucchini, shredded

- ½ cup apple, cored and shredded

- 5 tablespoons walnuts, chopped

For Topping:

- 1 tablespoon walnuts, chopped

- 2 teaspoons brown sugar

- ¼ teaspoon ground cinnamon

Instructions:

1. For bread: in a bowl, mix together the flour, baking powder, baking soda, cinnamon, and salt.

2. In another large bowl, mix well the oil, sugar, egg, and vanilla extract.

3. Add the flour mixture and mix until just combined.

4. Gently fold in the zucchini, apple and walnuts.

5. For the topping: in a small bowl, add all the ingredients and whisk them well.

6. Place the mixture into a lightly greased loaf pan and sprinkle with the topping mixture.

7. Select "Air Fry" of Breville Smart Air Fryer Oven and adjust the temperature to 325 degrees F.

8. Set the timer for 30 minutes and press "Start/Stop" to begin preheating.

9. When the unit beeps to show that it is preheated, arrange the loaf pan over the wire rack.

10. When the cooking time is complete, remove the loaf pan from oven and place the pan onto a wire rack to cool for about 10 minutes.

11. Carefully invert the bread onto the wire rack to cool completely before slicing.

12. Cut the bread into desired-sized slices and serve.

Carrot Bread

Servings: 6

Preparation Time: 15 minutes

Cooking Time: 30 minutes

Ingredients:

- 1 cup all-purpose flour

- 1 teaspoon baking soda

- ½ teaspoon ground cinnamon

- ¼ teaspoon ground cloves

- ¼ teaspoon ground nutmeg

- ½ teaspoon salt

- 2 large eggs

- ¾ cup vegetable oil

- 1/3 cup white sugar

- 1/3 cup light brown sugar

- ½ teaspoon vanilla extract

- 1½ cups carrots, peeled and grated

Instructions:

1. In a bowl, mix together the flour, baking soda, spices and salt.

2. In a large bowl, add the eggs, oil, sugars and vanilla extract and beat until well combined.

3. Add the flour mixture and mix until just combined.

4. Fold in the carrots.

5. Place the mixture into a lightly greased baking dish.

6. Select "Air Fry" of Breville Smart Air Fryer Oven and adjust the temperature to 320 degrees F.

7. Set the timer for 30 minutes and press "Start/Stop" to begin preheating.

8. When the unit beeps to show that it is preheated, arrange the baking dish over the wire rack and place onto a wire rack to cool for about 10 minutes.

9. Carefully invert the bread onto the wire rack to cool completely before slicing.

10. Cut the bread into desired-sized slices and serve.

Zucchini Fritters

Servings: 4

Preparation Time: 15 minutes

Cooking Time: 7 minutes

Ingredients:

- 10½ ounces zucchini, grated and squeezed

- 7 ounces Halloumi cheese

- ¼ cup all-purpose flour

- 2 eggs

- 1 teaspoon fresh dill, minced

- Salt and ground black pepper, as required

Instructions:

1. In a large bowl and mix together all the ingredients.

2. Make small-sized fritters from the mixture.

3. Arrange the fritters into the greased enamel roasting pan.

4. Select "Air Fry" of Breville Smart Air Fryer Oven and adjust the temperature to 355 degrees F.

5. Set the timer for 7 minutes and press "Start/Stop" to begin preheating.

6. When the unit beeps to show that it is preheated, insert the roasting pan in the oven.

7. When the cooking time is complete, remove the roasting pan from the oven.

8. Serve warm.

Pumpkin Pancakes

Servings: 4

Preparation Time: 15 minutes

Cooking Time: 12 minutes

Ingredients:

- 1 square puff pastry

- 3 tablespoons pumpkin filling

- 1 small egg, beaten

Instructions:

1. Roll out a puff pastry square and layer it with pumpkin pie filling, leaving about ¼-inch space around the edges.

2. Cut it up into 8 equal-sized square pieces and coat the edges with beaten egg.

3. Arrange the squares into the greased enamel roasting pan.

4. Select "Air Fry" of Breville Smart Air Fryer Oven and adjust the temperature to 355 degrees F.

5. Set the timer for 12 minutes and press "Start/Stop" to begin preheating.

6. When the unit beeps to show that it is preheated, insert the roasting pan in the oven.

7. When the cooking time is complete, remove the roasting pan from the oven.

8. Serve warm.

Nutella Banana Muffins

Servings: 12
Preparation Time: 15 minutes
Cooking Time: 25 minutes

Ingredients:

- 1 2/3 cups plain flour

- 1 teaspoon baking soda

- 1 teaspoon baking powder

- 1 teaspoon ground cinnamon

- ¼ teaspoon salt

- 4 ripe bananas, peeled and mashed

- 2 eggs

- ½ cup brown sugar

- 1 teaspoon vanilla essence

- 3 tablespoons milk

- 1 tablespoon Nutella

- ¼ cup walnuts

Instructions:

1. Grease 12 muffin molds. Set aside.

2. In a large bowl, sift together the flour, baking soda, baking powder, cinnamon, and salt.

3. In another bowl, mix together the remaining ingredients except for walnuts.

4. Add the banana mixture into the flour mixture and mix until just combined.

5. Fold in the walnuts.

6. Place the mixture into the prepared muffin molds.

7. Select "Air Fry" of Breville Smart Air Fryer Oven and adjust the temperature to 250 degrees F.

8. Set the timer for 25 minutes and press "Start/Stop" to begin preheating.

9. When the unit beeps to show that it is preheated, arrange the muffin molds over the wire rack.

10. When the cooking time is complete, remove the muffin molds from oven and set aside to cool for about 10 minutes.

11. Carefully invert the muffins onto the wire rack to completely

Conclusion

The Breville Smart Air Fryer Oven will help you cook everything that you want to serve at the table. Whether you are serving a large family gathering or cooking food, your homies, this kitchen miracle will help you cook all the portion sizes in just a few minutes. So, to buy all the different cooking appliances when you can replace them all with a single appliance which is simple to use and efficient in working. And if you have already made up your mind about the Breville Smart Air Fryer Oven, then this cookbook can be your perfect cooking partner as it will give you all the smart cooking secrets that you need to use this machine up to its full potential.